# WILLIAM YEOWARD
on
# ENTERTAINING

# WILLIAM YEOWARD
## on
# ENTERTAINING

photography PAUL RYAN

CICO BOOKS

LONDON  NEW YORK

*For Ruth, who was very wise*

Published in 2008 by CICO Books
An imprint of Ryland Peters & Small

20–21 Jockey's Fields
London WC1R 4BW

5th Floor 519 Broadway,
New York, NY 10012

10 9 8 7 6 5 4 3 2

Text © William Yeoward 2008
Design and photography © CICO Books 2008

A CIP catalog record for this book is available from the Library of
Congress and the British Library.

ISBN-13: 978 1 906094 62 1

Printed in China

Editor: Gillian Haslam
Additional text: Posy Gentles
Designer: Christine Wood

# Contents

# Introduction

For most of us, the very word "entertaining" is enough to send us into a flat spin and cause us to become short of breath! It seems to me that we are so conditioned by the fear of organizing the party that we totally forget that having a gathering is meant to be an enjoyable and fun experience, rather than some alarming endurance course we have set for ourselves.

I suggest that one always remembers never to commit to something that, even at the outset, you suspect is going to cause you terrible anxiety later! I, of course, do not always follow my own advice.

In this, my second book, I want to illustrate that entertaining is a very broad word for seeing one's friends and family. I love gathering people up from all walks of life for some specific celebration. A mix is always preferable because it's so nice for guests when they don't know everyone at a party and nearly everyone enjoys meeting new people.

From a spring wedding for two hundred guests to the winegrower's lunch for four, this book serves to show how various occasions and events can be themed to suit the location, table setting, and menu.

The locations within these pages have been chosen not only because they represent a cross-section of the marvelous places that I visit when traveling, but also how "global" entertaining can be. Whether on a farm in Virginia, a beautiful old Hollywood house, or a finca in Spain, an atmosphere can be created that is not only special to the place but also gives the occasion a real feeling of identity.

Food is such an important part of entertaining—and certainly I adore cooking—and the idea of a constant flow of visitors gives me a feeling not of panic, but of great joy. This I would like to share in these pages.

Having confidence and a sense of humor is of absolute paramount importance when entertaining, and it really doesn't matter at all what goes on behind the scenes as long as the result is pleasing and the party a success! I remember a terrible time at home when my dear dog Poppy brought in something inexcusable from the garden and dumped it in front of my stove. The next thing I knew was the salmon that I was hauling out of the oven went flying across the room with me attached and "swam" across the floor, settling very unhappily in a corner, not, of course, in a very complete or presentable state! The fish was meant to cool and be served with a fabulous concoction of roasted potatoes mixed with roasted Amalfi lemons, developed by my friend Karen. Needless to say, the fish had to be reconfigured into fishcakes! Such is life and such is entertaining.

I truly love entertaining and hope you will enjoy this book and feel inspired by the hugely varied locations that I have chosen to illustrate my genuine enthusiasm for this age-old occupation.

William Yeoward

# CHAPTER ONE

# Formal Entertaining

# Penthouse Supper

This apartment is beautifully and subtly decorated in a neutral palette, so introducing a riot of color to this table would have been thoroughly inappropriate. However, I wanted to create a table with texture and interest that would provide a perfect platform to enhance the food laid upon it.

A starkly monochromatic approach would have been harsh and cold—not at all conducive to bonhomie or enjoying your

LEFT AND ABOVE: The boldness of the candelabra with their rock crystal leaves and hand-forged bronze trunks gave me a vehicle on which to hang the composition of this delightfully contemporary arrangement.

LEFT: The style in which you choose to fold your napkins adds immediate impact to a table. I favor a simple fold or roll, so that the napkin looks ready for use, rather than elaborate creations of waterlilies or fans. A plain band with a decorative motif is all that's needed to ornament the striking black-and-white stripes.

BELOW: Topaz-colored crystal fruits contain olive oil and balsamic vinegar. These are gorgeous table decorations with a strong and real purpose.

BELOW RIGHT: A trip to the haberdashers or notions store can often fuel me with the inspiration and tools to embellish and adorn any napkin.

supper. My secret for this stunning, apparently black-and-white table setting is the use of dull greens, soft grays, taupes, and creams. The effect is of a soft gleam rather than a brilliant sparkle. I have avoided using too much glittering crystal, preferring the gentler play of light on white frosted glasses and roundly ridged glass vases. Variation in texture softens the mood further with the grayish-black of the wooden table and the silvery gleam of the flatware. The use of pattern is subtle but dynamic, pairing the strong stripe of the napkins with the squares and dots of the china.

I love to bring different styles together. I abhor too much uniformity, which can be sterile and unimaginative. Here I've used traditional flatware with 1950s-inspired plates and modern glass. Color and effect, rather than period consistency, have been my guiding principles.

LEFT: The delicate purple veining on the white petals of the orchid intensifies as it reaches the central speckled purple lip. They look beautiful when coupled together with some simple lilies (right).

RIGHT: Contrasts bring vivacity to a table. These acid-etched glasses with clear panels provide an elegant and geometric foil to the organic shape of the rounded vases while picking up the pure white of the lilies.

# menu

Roasted Portobello mushrooms
with Roquefort on a bed of polenta
and baby spinach

Seared Barbary duck breasts on a
ragoût of Puy lentils

Chocolate delice,
served with freshly sliced Alfonso mango

LEFT AND RIGHT: My friend Colin, who makes
me delicious studio vases, came up with the
perfect shades of abstract color: no black,
no brown, no white, no gray—simply beauty,
sparkle, and lashings of modern glamour.

# City Dining

ABOVE LEFT: It's all about razzle-dazzle. Glamorous crystal and a transparent splendor add much to the razzmatazz of this table setting.

ABOVE RIGHT: The floral element is pared down to simple white roses, and the arrangement is repeated with precise geometric formality.

LEFT: A minimalist dining room inspired this tailored setting. A strict palette of white and lime on a generously polished table is illuminated by a glittering array of crystal vases and elegant shaded candlesticks.

I love to open my cabinet full of the gorgeous things I adore using, fling back the doors, and face the challenge of pulling out something fabulously fresh, unusual, and different.

My friend was entertaining for the last time in her house before moving and I wanted to make this a stunning occasion that would never be forgotten. My imagination soared as I considered how to make a white theme work in an entirely new and unexpected way. I thought of lime, white, and sparkle in spades—I love sparkle!

This was a table for people of fine taste and elegant lifestyle so the emphasis would obviously have to be very grown-up. I believe that the success of any party is vastly increased by the thought and attention given to the table and the menu. I pictured guests relaxing and chatting as the food was served, marveling at the fantastic quality and luster of the crystal and flowers.

Chic simplicity set the tone. First, I considered the flowers. I felt a pantomime of color would not be the way to go, so I went to the opposite extreme of using only one type of flower, an exquisite, closely petaled, creamy white rose. Bunched at high level and single at low level, the display has a pleasing symmetry, with the green stems showing through the crystal, adding to the harmony of the table. I kept the table low so that the sparkling flow of conversation should not be hindered by having to peer around towering vases or candlesticks.

On these formal occasions, I often find myself veering toward the smart restraint of a gleaming polished wood surface. To me, tablecloths seem more appropriate for multi-generational parties.

TOP LEFT AND BOTTOM LEFT: The delicious and seasonal menu for this midsummer dinner (see page 25) echoes the lime-green theme on display perfectly.

CENTER LEFT: Facet-cutting on crystal is always so pleasing to the eye in its geometric simplicity.

RIGHT: Like soldiers in a regiment, everything on the table must be in the right place, lined up properly. In certain established households, among them Her Majesty Queen Elizabeth's, a ruler may even be used to ensure everything is spot on.

# menu

Gently chilled watercress soup,
with a swirl of crème fraîche, served in
lidded cups and saucers à la Française

Roasted salmon with ouzo and capers

Fava bean and mint purée

Pink rose-petal ice cream,
scattered with crystalized petals, served in tall
stemmed crystal with almond biscuits

LEFT: I chose a white theme for this table, but made
it work in a new and unexpected way. Lime, white,
and sparkle in spades!

ABOVE: The perfection of a single white rose needs
no fancy foliage.

**25**

LEFT: I adore the naturalness of these arrangements of blossom. With scarcely a modicum of florist's talent, one can go into the garden, cut great swathes of blossom, and thrust them into pots. Et voila!

RIGHT: Delectably thin sweet toasts are delicious with champagne. Again, pretty simplicity was my guiding principle here.

FAR RIGHT: Perfect, shining crystal glasses were ranked on plain cream linen mats placed on a pleasing slab of slate.

## menu

Champagne

Champagne citron pressé

Bellini

Joe's refresher

Elderflower and lemongrass tea

Sweet toasts

# Wedding Cocktails

Isn't it every girl's dream to be married in springtime under a bower of blossom? At my friend's family home nestled in American farmland, I gathered armfuls of cherry blossom to make this dream come true.

We chose the charming potting shed to welcome the wedding guests with cocktails. I say shed, for this is its purpose, yet the building has height, elegance, and style. Amid the over-arching sprays of blossom a congenial, informal mood was created. The guests relaxed and chatted to new and old friends, enjoying champagne and cocktails.

The sense of occasion was set with the gleaming clarity of the crystal and the untouched branches of palest pink blossom. There was not a hint of opulent decadence here; all was natural, pure, and youthful as befits a family wedding. When the moment for the ceremony arrived, the guests walked the few steps to the garden pavilion where the wedding was to take place.

# Spring Wedding

The marriage vows were taken in a small pavilion, simply furnished with a beautiful old linen cloth and a few sprays of cherry blossom. This wedding was held at the family home, using garden flowers and family possessions handed down through generations. This is befitting to an occasion when two families are joined together and gives an intensely personal atmosphere to the proceedings.

Adjacent to the pavilion is the clapboard garden room where the wedding breakfast was laid out. The solemnity of the ceremony gave way to feasting, much talking, reminiscing for the older members of the party perhaps, and much hilarity, no doubt, for the children who escaped to play in the garden when permitted.

LEFT: I decorated all the tables in a similar way, with flowers soaring to the ceiling to make full use of the height of the garden room, and offering no hindrance to the easy flow of conversation.

ABOVE: The open-sided pavilion needed no elaborate floral artistry when the garden was in view all around. Nature was allowed to do her job and I was grateful to her.

On a personal occasion such as a wedding, don't let yourself be bullied by erroneous ideas of coordination. Use treasured and beautiful things where you can. I loathe seeing the wedding breakfast decked out in hired glasses, plates, and flatware just for the sake of uniformity, like a conference dinner in a business hotel.

Use flowers and color to give coherence to your theme. I adored the rich green of a length of antique silk velvet and threw it over the top table. As I added to the table, pinks, golds, and greengage shades of green were soon singing against the sumptuous fabric, the gold detail of the eighteenth-century plates, the shining crystal and family silver, the pink rose petals, delicate blossom, and the fresh green mopheads of the hydrangeas. I also dyed intricately embroidered linen napkins a soft greengage for the occasion—it's fun to do something that's unique and special.

ABOVE: I believe there is an intense relationship between food and flowers. Here, soft pink rose petals provide a pleasing echo to the artifice of the frosted rose on the cake.

ABOVE LEFT: To my mind, the pastel shades and white that are so often chosen for weddings can verge on the clinical, whereas this table has warmth and individuality.

RIGHT: A simple yet perfect sprig of cherry blossom from the garden is the only decoration this place setting needs.

There is an intense beauty in the juxtaposition of the elements on the serving table. Strings of pearls tumble into cherry blossom. Meringues are cradled in crystal comports and adorned with petals. Rich red strawberries glow through crystal, and black-purple grapes cascade. The beauty of the food is essential: the deep pinks, reds, and purples of the fruit, the rich depth of the chocolate, and the ephemeral lightness of the meringues. Wedding food must work with the ambience. It must be simple, beautiful, and classy. Above all, it must be informally enjoyed.

I strove to infuse this display with passion. The possibilities for effusive decoration are boundless. Forget restricting convention—a wedding is an opportunity when everything may still not be enough.

RIGHT: The delicate prettiness of this comport of meringues and rose petals shows again the gorgeous symbiosis that exists between food and flowers.

BELOW LEFT: Perfectly simple champagne flutes and dripping pearls are deliciously elegant.

BELOW: The bitterness of the chocolate marries perfectly with the sweet aromatic red of the raspberries, both in taste and appearance.

# menu

Salmon and scallop blinis with sour cream,
garnished with lashings of caviar

Roasted lobster with lemon risotto
Watercress and shredded fennel salad

Strawberry roulade
Bitter chocolate and raspberry tatin
Brown sugar meringues and clotted cream
laced with orange

Iced cheese soufflé

LEFT AND RIGHT: **Continuing the theme
of spring blossom from the potting shed,
I added only lime-white hydrangeas and
scented pink roses touched with lime to
create a symphony of color—greengage,
lime, and pink balanced by the underlying
theme of the velvet cloth.**

# Family Gathering

Sunday lunch with my relations is always fun and informal. We retell old family stories, interrupting and embellishing, quibbling good-humoredly about details that would seem to be of paltry significance. I bring out the same beautiful dinner service that the older of us remember from childhood; use the same chairs where, as children, we were admonished for wriggling and being silly. We, as adults, gently admonish the present generation of children sitting on the same chairs. Such is the glorious continuity of family life.

ABOVE: I love going out into the garden once the cooking is under control and choosing flowers for a gathering like this. These ranunculus and hellebores are informal but very pretty.

RIGHT: This early nineteenth-century stoneware dinner service has already served five generations and so has a value to the family that is far beyond its intrinsic beauty.

# menu

Cornish crab bisque

Roast fillet of beef on a bed of
blanched summer vegetables with
béarnaise sauce

Millefeuille with lemon cream
Baked Alaska with rhubarb
compote

LEFT: While you preserve the past,
give a thought to the future. These
gorgeous cobalt glasses will be the
treasures of generations to come.

41

Setting your table with all that is old, loved, and handed-down brings intense familiarity to the occasion, throwing up many affectionate memories of those who live on in the family spirit.

As you look through your cabinets, you may be tempted to give a Gallic shrug and sigh "Autres temps, autres moeurs" (other times, other ways). Fruit knives and crystal rinsers may seem superfluous in this more casual, less thrifty age, but if a piece is still beautiful, I like to use it and find it another purpose.

Rinsers with a lip either side were once provided for guests to rinse out their wine glass between different wines. I admired the simplicity of the crystal and floated an umbel of cow parsley in each to adorn my place settings, while fruit knives are perfect for bread and butter.

I adore the attainability of entertaining like this—using your own possessions and a little imagination to create a beautiful table.

TOP LEFT: The emphatic deep pinks of the ranunculus glow against the citrus green of the hellebores and give vibrance to this brilliant table.

BOTTOM LEFT: Never mind the dishwasher! When you have family around, there are plenty of hands to help with the dishwashing. It is the time to bring out Granny's silver. These enchantingly old ebony-handled fruit knives are reincarnated as butter knives.

RIGHT: The rough, vintage-linen cloth for this table has been used for an age. Its informality encapsulates the ambience of this family gathering and is a perfect background for the cow parsley.

# A Southern Dinner

It's early summer in the southern states of America and my friends are holding a dinner party. It is to be a family meeting of adults and, because this is a household of the traditional South, the love of home and family expresses itself in formality as well as affection and warmth. The double doors open on to a scene of calm and dignity. There is nothing modern to be found here. From the golden twinkling of the chandelier to the perfectly smooth white damask tablecloth, the atmosphere speaks of quality, permanence, and, above all, a great pride in tradition.

I encapsulated that sense of timelessness with copious quantities of candles. The table is lit almost entirely by candlelight and its gentle flicker can be seen from the wall sconces and the hurricane shades on the beautiful painted serving table.

LEFT: As you open the double doors to the dining room, you find warm golden candlelight and a scene that has changed little in the past two hundred years.

ABOVE: The grandeur of the family pieces is charmingly offset by small vases of modest but very pretty flowers, such as these sweet peas and snakeshead fritillaries.

45

The table is set with family possessions that have been handed down through generations. I looked for pieces that would gleam, shimmer, and reflect the flickering golden light of the many candles.

Luster china was the lead for the whole table and I added elegant, highly polished old family silver and shining, mismatched wine glasses. The purple and pink ranunculus, sweet peas, and snakeshead fritillaries picked up the colors in the luster plates.

The damask tablecloth and knife-edge creased, gorgeously embroidered napkins completed this traditional picture.

## menu

Louisiana lump crabmeat with
old-fashioned Green Goddess dressing

Braised quail with cheese grits soufflé
Salad of greens and herbs with spicy
pecans and vinaigrette

Little shortcakes with garden
strawberries and whipped cream

BELOW LEFT: **Perfectly polished family silver gleams golden in the candlelight.**

BELOW CENTER: **Vases of deep pink ranunculus add a vivid dash of brilliance to the table.**

BELOW RIGHT: **The fabulous quality of the old crystal gives the appearance of custom and decorum.**

RIGHT: **Formality reigns and the family's monogramed napkins are well starched and sharply folded.**

I love to light lots of candles and position them so that they reflect as much as possible. The mirrored wall sconces shown here give double the impact. Stand candles in front of wall mirrors and put them inside glass shades so that they glint and shine through. Place your candles at different heights so that the source of light is further diffused, and try using colored glass receptacles to give a background glow.

Here I used antique cranberry glasses for tealights. However, if you are relying on candles as your main source of light, limit your use of colored glass because it dims the illumination (that, of course, can sometimes be rather a good thing!)

ABOVE: A single candle is given extra impact as it glints and glimmers through a highly polished hurricane shade.

LEFT: Place candles in front of mirrors and at different heights to achieve a diffused golden glow.

CHAPTER TWO

# Teatime Entertaining

# Granny's Birthday Tea

LEFT: I chose these delicately engraved champagne saucers rather than the flutes often favored today as a nod to nostalgic glamour.

BELOW: The prettiest, whitest, starched napkins were absolutely essential on this occasion to please eagle-eyed guests with traditionally high standards for such things. Scalloped edges and delicate embroidery are perfection.

Tea is a fabulous meal for our older relatives—it suits their metabolism! I set up this tea table in the drawing room for the birthday of my American friend's grandmother. This gave the celebration intimacy and comfort, which, in my experience, is what grandmothers like.

I set a scene of old-fashioned prettiness and ease, using an ivory silk quilted counterpane as a tablecloth, liberally and traditionally decorated with pale pink roses arranged singly and in pairs in small glass vases.

I chose well-upholstered chairs with arms because I suspected this little celebratory tea could cheerfully turn to cocktails as the evening drew in. Champagne corks would

be popped and all the old girls would have a lively, giggly time and would need to be comfortably settled in.

So that there should be no awkwardness among the guests as to whether cocktails were a possibility or not, I boldly set out prettily engraved champagne saucers at each place so that pleasant expectation should reign while tea and cakes were served.

A sparkling candelabra made a wonderful centerpiece encircled by silver candlesticks, so that the flickering light came from different heights to radiate *joie de vivre*.

# menu

Trout and horseradish sandwiches
Chicken and sweet smoked paprika sandwiches

Lemon and blueberry waffles
Twice-baked chocolate cookies
Coconut cream cake

Darjeeling and Orange Pekoe tea

Champagne

TOP LEFT: Champagne and pink roses have an old-fashioned glamour that is just right for an elderly lady's tea party.

LEFT: I love to make guests feel special and placed little gift boxes beside each setting, charmingly illustrated with old flower prints.

RIGHT: The highly textured table covering is a perfect background to the simple beauty of the pink roses.

# Pink Tea Party

This gorgeous baroque-style pink tea party is an example of me indulging myself! The table is for that precious snap of time when friends call unexpectedly and one is suddenly inspired to set the table with really beautiful things, just to celebrate the pleasure of the moment.

My favorite flower is the rose and I worship this rose china, which radiates extravagant luxury. This occasion sees me pulling treasured items from the back of cabinets, arranging them randomly and beautifully over the table, to be admired by guests.

Add a flower in a small vase, finely cut sandwiches, a delicious tart or two, and the perfect pot of tea. These are the staples of the English tea party and one needs no more.

LEFT: The art of silver-gilding on porcelain was very fashionable in eighteenth-century France and has recently enjoyed a modest renaissance among contemporary ceramicists. It's a nice twist on the stuffy English tradition.

ABOVE: This silver teapot has been in the family for years.

# menu

Perfect cucumber sandwiches with
chopped watercress and cream cheese

Lemon meringue tart
Slices of home-baked fruit loaf

A pot of tea, to taste:
Lapsang Souchong, Earl Grey,
English Breakfast, or Assam

LEFT: Pink as a palette and art-form lends itself so well to tea-drinking.

BELOW AND RIGHT: These gorgeously decorated pieces look almost as if they have been frosted. They always remind me of the beauty of the English garden in early summer.

# Children's Fun

BELOW: Cutting fresh flowers from your garden is an exciting way to spark off ideas for color schemes. The fresh lime-green of the alchemilla mollis froths around the apricot of the roses and the burnished orange of the chrysanthemums. Add a stunning Schiaparelli-pink table mat and a deeper accent of amethyst in your glasses.

For a children's party I always provide masses of color, fun, excitement, and surprises, such as the opportunity to take on a new identity for a few hours and, of course, to leave laden with presents.

I like to think one can take a theme and hang a party on it. Most children can sing a verse or two of "Nelly the Elephant" and will be irresistibly

drawn to this brilliantly colored table. There is much to entertain them: an elephant for each child to play with and take home, colorful masks, and a box of treasures at each place to be investigated. I notice sadly that the days of offering sandwiches first, cake last, are long gone. But it's the way of the world and there's little use fighting against it.

BELOW: The vivid, joyful colors of this table setting are shouting "Party." The beautiful masks wait to be donned, the crackers to be noisily and hilariously pulled, and the jewel-like glasses to be filled to the brim.

# menu

Always include a nice, sticky chocolate cake, delicious tarts, and cookies

Apple or cranberry spritzer

Few, if any, sensible savories (sadly)

# Eating
# Ice Cream

I was sitting in the garden, trying to read the Sunday newspaper. I had been at a show in Paris and arrived home in the early hours. Poppy, my dog, evidently deciding this was not the grand reunion she had been expecting, was doing her best to stop me.

Still, it was a sunny June afternoon. The delphiniums and foxgloves were in full bloom, my chair was comfortable, and I had nothing (except the endeavors of Poppy) to make me get out of it. Then my telephone rang.

It was some dear friends driving through Gloucestershire, deciding to ring on a whim to see if they could call on me. Pleased, I agreed immediately they must come. I put the phone down, then realized that I hadn't been shopping, there was no time to shop before they arrived, and my only milk had been so horribly curdled that I had thrown it away.

So, no tea then. Champagne? No, they were driving.

Then, to my great satisfaction, I remembered that I had a lot of rather delicious ice cream in different flavors stashed in the freezer. I'd bought it a couple of weeks before at a farm that had rightly won several awards for making the stuff. I tossed my newspaper to the mercy of Poppy, and set to work to create an ice-cream feast in twenty-five minutes.

LEFT: Over the years, I've collected many and various pieces of fabric to use as tablecloths. A length of floaty Indian gauze was perfect for an ice-cream party in the garden, and the ceramic spoons and matching dishes echo the colors.

RIGHT: A garden full of delphiniums and foxgloves is the perfect setting for eating ice cream.

In a matter of minutes, I flung a length of sequinned Indian silk over my garden table, cut a few flowers, and found some rather charming ceramic ice-cream dishes and spoons that I'd bought in Italy.

I chose red roses just because their gorgeous color caught my eye as I was dashing around with my pruning shears. Then I noticed that opening buds of my pink peonies looked just like balls of strawberry ice cream. Well, you know I can never resist a visual pun, so snip, snip, and into a dish they went.

BELOW: Bringing the garden to the table: a dish of pink peonies and red roses, and drinks embellished with sprigs of mint.

BELOW LEFT: An ice-cold flagon of home-made lemonade is very efficient at cooling you down on a hot June day.

BELOW: Each Italian ceramic ice-cream dish has its matching ceramic spoon. I preferred to mix up the colors.

BELOW RIGHT: Keep an open mind as you set your table. Often an inspired impulse, like this belljar, can become the *pièce de résistance*.

I snatched a few sprigs of mint to add to the home-made lemonade. I'm an expert at this and can make a jug up in five minutes flat. The ice cream, of course, needed no preparation.

As I was squeezing lemons, a glass belljar that we love but has never yet quite found its home caught my eye and suddenly seemed to me incredibly reminiscent of old-fashioned ice-cream parlors. I placed it over a vase of flowers as an instant centerpiece to the table. And then the doorbell rang.

# menu

Home-made lemonade
with sprigs of fresh mint

Ice cream:
Blueberry parfait
Kiwi and lime sorbet
Thyme sorbet
Mango sherbet
Raspberry sherbet
Mint tea sherbet
Vanilla bean ice cream
Spiced chocolate ice cream

Home-baked Madeira cake

LEFT: A perfectly simple small white
linen table mat adds that touch of
ice-cream parlor finesse.

RIGHT: The choice of many and varied
flavors of ice creams, sorbets, and
sherbets does bring out the child in
people, I find.

# A
# Lover Calls

Imagine the velvety tones of Ella Fitzgerald singing "I love Paris" and slide into the mood of this romantic scene.

Picture a gentle awakening, sensuous and soft in fine poplin sheets and a silk eiderdown, as your lover sets down a tray on the bed. First, the unexpected joy of seeing your lover, and then the unfolding delights of the tray.

The details are thoughtfully affectionate rather than expensive, impersonal statements: the inscribed ceramic hearts, the few carefully chosen flowers tied with a green ribbon, the charming embroidered traycloth. The color scheme of lilac and moss-green is taken from the delicately painted tea cups.

When you make a romantic gesture, you needn't break the bank. Thought and care is so much more intimate and expressive.

Throw your money instead at the plane ticket to Paris, artfully concealed beneath the postcard of the Eiffel Tower.

## menu

Cup of tea
Plane ticket

TOP LEFT: There must always be flowers. This posy of orchids, sweet peas, and delphiniums is a harmony of blue, lilac, and deep magenta.

BELOW LEFT: These whimsically inscribed ceramic hearts are amusing, charming, and intimate.

RIGHT: A cup of tea in bed is surely one of life's great pleasures. And how that cup runneth over when the thoughtfully decorated tray reveals a plane ticket to Paris.

CHAPTER THREE

# Entertaining at the Pool

# Groovy Poolside

The bliss of the informal is that you can work organically with your surroundings and create something unique and special. As long as there is congeniality, comfort, and delicious food, anything is possible. I threw convention out of the window for this Californian pool party. With gusto I threw the doors open and demolished the boundary between inside and out.

Sometimes you can dispense with formality completely. This groovy poolside party was all about friendship and laughter. Palm trees, sunshine, intense color, and a great feeling of well being were my inspiration. Too formal a lunch and the mood would have been spoilt. As it was, after eating, guests returned seamlessly to their splashy pleasures and the party continued.

ABOVE: The appropriateness of engraved palm trees on the crystal was irresistible for this party.

LEFT: Bright scarves used as tablecloths, colored crystal, and piles of freshly gathered salad bring the vibrant intensity of Californian sunshine to the lunch table.

I turned my back on flowers without a second thought, preferring to adorn the table with the salad and vegetables we would later eat. The device of getting guests to prepare their own salad created a cheerful and noisy atmosphere, just right for this lively party. Sweet-juiced tomatoes were exchanged for aniseed-scented slices of fennel. I couldn't swear that the odd lemon wasn't pitched from one end of the table to the other!

The freshness and scent of locally gathered Californian produce was adored by the guests at this table, perfectly echoing the mood of zest for outdoor activity and hedonistic healthy pleasures.

## menu

Salad of decorative table center!

Chermoula chicken skewers
Piri piri tuna burgers
Rough-cut, blackened smoked ham

Tray-baked rosemary and sage focaccia

The freshest fruit

LEFT: Unconventional, groovy, and gorgeous!

RIGHT: Just-picked salads are healthy, delicious, and make a fabulously funky table center, obliterating the distinction between decoration and lunch.

BELOW: Where vivid color is paramount and rules are to be broken, funky plastic knives and forks, jokey napkins, and expensive crystal work together beautifully.

BELOW RIGHT: Bringing the outside in: the blue of the swimming-pool and the fresh greens of young leaves are reflected throughout my color scheme.

RIGHT: Illuminated by the Californian sunshine, the crystal glasses in jewel colors of amber, cobalt, amethyst, and ruby became dazzling in their intensity.

My only rule here was to make it look fabulous. The gloves were off—I wanted full-on hot color, totally inspired by the environment, and I wasn't going to stand on ceremony. The mood was funky, frivolous, and fun. I mixed kitsch plastic knives and forks in brilliant purples, greens, and blues with handmade crystal in jewel colors. I chose napkins embroidered with brightly colored lobsters and ice-cream sundaes—vulgar in another context, perfect here. I indulged shamelessly in visual puns: the palm trees engraved on the expensive crystal, the splashy patterns of the scarves. The blazing Californian sunshine poured through the wide-open doors, glancing and piercing through the jewel colors of the crystal.

# Lunch
# at the Poolhouse

The Magnolia stellata bursts forth its abundant spidery white flowers and spring has come to England's Home Counties. It's time to put your nose out of the door and enjoy those first traces of warmth and sunshine. It's still too cold to eat *al fresco* but how delicious to set up lunch in a beautiful building in the garden that you have visited little during the short, dark days of winter—a summer house maybe or, as we have here, the poolhouse.

ABOVE: A woven basket packed with all the ingredients for a garden table.

RIGHT: The perfect early spring setting for an intimate lunch for four friends.

The size of the building dictates that this will be an intimate lunch, in this case for four good friends. There is an element of picnicking here—you will need to pack your basket with provisions, but you need not stint on the beauty of your table, which can be set earlier. Think Marie Antoinette rather than Girl Guides!

Here the round table has been covered with a thick, cream, vintage-linen cloth, which complements the seat covers. It is laid with classic blue-and-white china, set off to perfection by pure white roses. Subtle color contrasts are added with the antique green-handled flatware and the cream checked napkins. The clean lines of the glasses and flagons enhance the simplicity of the table and underline the informality of lunch with old friends.

BELOW LEFT: Pure white roses, blue-and-white china, and glass flagons never fail to please.

BELOW: I have provided two napkins as fish is to be eaten. The double-layered effect is as attractive as it is practical.

RIGHT: I like to use contrasts in my settings. The slubby vintage-linen tablecloth used here emphasizes the clean blue and white of the china and the sparkle of the crystal.

LEFT: This old green-handled flatware is very special and I adore it. As well as that, it adds a different color to the table.

BELOW LEFT: The country loaf of bread wrapped in a dish towel contrasts with the elegance of the china and classic white roses.

RIGHT: The first course, as well as tasting delicious, must look beautiful. It is the first view of the table. By the time the second course arrives, guests will be immersed in chat.

# menu

Amuse-gueules of salted cod

Sausages: duck, venison, chicken
Roast new potato salad with dill pickles
and Dijon mustard mayonnaise

Sliced blood oranges with bitter chocolate mousse

# An Evening at the Pool

My friends' beautiful poolside at their house in southern Spain always reminds me of Daisy when she first sees Gatsby's shirts in Fitzgerald's novel: "Shirts with stripes and scrolls and plaids …"

Maybe I think of *The Great Gatsby* because of the elegant furnishings—stripes and scrolls and plaids in shades of blue—or maybe it's the achievement of the dream: the dream we work so hard to achieve.

Nothing in this calm scene is in any way demanding or aggressive. I know this sounds paradoxical, but I see this as smart casual without the smart or casual.

LEFT: Shades of blue against the natural yellows of stone and wood create a perfectly tranquil scene for sinking into a delectably cold cocktail after a day in the sun and before a delicious supper.

We may spend the day walking in the hills, visiting the sights, or shopping for local specialties. Then it's back to the finca, a splash in the pool, a shower, and a clean white linen shirt and cocktails!

Lazy from the warmth of the Spanish sun, with the pleasant enticement of the pool always in front of you (to be taken up again—or not!), you can relax as an ice-cold drink is gently placed in your hand.

## menu

Salted nuts
Local black olives

Cruzcampo beer
Ice-cold fino or manzanilla sherry

LEFT: Cocktail hour in hot countries is heaven: a shower and fresh clothes with the warmth of the sun still glowing on your skin, the expectation of a delicious supper, and an ice-cold cocktail to relax with by the pool.

TOP RIGHT: Don't go overboard with salty snacks. To my mind, a few bitter black olives and salted nuts are perfection. A handful of flowering sage plucked from the garden is a simple yet charming touch.

RIGHT: Keep a selection of glasses to hand. Make sure beers are in the refrigerator and there's plenty of ice.

# The Long Days of Summer

This is outdoor living at its most luxurious and grown-up. The blue-and-white textiles—vintage linens, striped cottons, faded denims—have an unruffled masculine glamour, and an organic quality in this context of cloudless skies and rippling pool.

My friends have a great *laissez-faire* attitude to entertaining in their holiday home. We spend the day as we please, lounging by the pool or setting off on expeditions. In the evening we sit down together for a lively supper, which one of us will have prepared. I love going to the local markets and picking up fresh vegetables and fish, or a pungent local cheese.

ABOVE: The calm, uncomplicated checks and stripes in blue hues exude an air of pared-down masculinity.

RIGHT: A bolthole of cool blue serenity nestling in the arid Spanish mountains.

LEFT: The gentle swaying of the pure white cotton drapes, simply trimmed with a clean blue stripe, creates an ephemeral and shifting boundary between the supper table and the pool outside.

RIGHT: The table is glimpsed through the drapes. Even such a slight boundary is very effective. I enjoy supper with friends and I enjoy lounging by the pool, but don't want to do both at the same time!

# menu

Globe artichoke with anchoïade

Vitello tonnato con capperi
Leaf salad with lemon dressing

Almond tart with grilled white peaches

ABOVE: For this table, I have kept each setting within the confines of the place mat to maintain that sense of unruffled order.

LEFT: Great earthenware pots of viburnum and fennel bring the outside in and contrast pleasingly with the strict formality of the place settings.

**101**

A fresh white linen shirt, shorts, and comfortable flip-flops are *de rigueur* for this supper. Formality in this case is only a means to keep things uncomplicated.

The first course of locally grown artichokes is already on the table. In this atmosphere, I like to have the first course placed on the table before guests are seated. The authority of the cook is dispensed with, cocktails can be finished at leisure, and there is no haste or pressure.

My choice of glasses, plates, and table linen reflects this uncluttered haven: stripes, checks, little ornamentation. All is clean, pure, and beautiful.

BELOW: Lemons picked from a tree in the garden and pots of feathery aromatic fennel stand on an ancient stone sink.

BELOW LEFT: The many textures play off each other in a harmony of blue and white.

RIGHT: Local artichokes, to be enjoyed with piquant anchoïade, await the guests, who are enjoying their cocktails in the evening sun. The tyranny of food is certainly not welcome here!

CHAPTER FOUR

# Entertaining Outdoors

# Down on the Farm

The bliss of setting up your table on a veranda is the satisfying of an immediate urge to eat outside, of pulling things out of the house as soon as the opportunity presents itself. I adore eating outside, so I was delighted when, while staying with American friends in the Carolinas, a lovely spring evening coincided with the first cutting of the season's asparagus.

This supper was about seizing that moment and enjoying it. I set the table for a few close friends to gorge on asparagus while enjoying a glorious view of spring blossom, lines of post-and-rail fences, and fields misting into the distance.

ABOVE: The familiarity of old possessions—a straw hat, a checkered napkin, the rush-seated chair— set the mood for this comfortable scene.

RIGHT: The painted veranda, scrubbed table, and weathered chairs are the perfect setting from which to enjoy the view of fertile Carolina farmland.

This was an informal, spur-of-the-moment supper with the glasses, plates, and table linen brought out from the house and a bunch of scented white lilac hastily cut from the garden. The staples of the meal were likewise simple and thrown together but of fabulous quality—freshly cut asparagus, a home-made sourdough loaf still warm from the kitchen oven, garden-grown salad leaves. Eating asparagus within an hour of cutting ranks among the principal joys of the epicure. It is a meal best enjoyed tête-à-tête, where no-one cares if you eat with your hands, dripping butter, and making liberal use of your napkin.

In my book, informal never so much as verges on the slapdash. I take inspiration from the occasion. Here I chose the delicate greens and purples of the asparagus to create the table. A linen table runner, faded to the softest lilac, was thrown across the scrubbed top. Lilac and cream checkered napkins, rustically fringed, were simply folded on the green lettuce-leaf plates.

The rich purple of the grapes, to be eaten with good salty mountain cheese, were decorative in their own right, held aloft on a tazza. Unembellished water glasses completed this rustic scene.

TOP LEFT: A beautiful view like this doesn't need the distraction of an elaborate table.

LEFT: The lilac and green color scheme was inspired by the colors of the asparagus.

RIGHT: I always try to keep a store of palate-stimulators, such as these dried wasabi peas. They look rather gorgeous with the lilac, too.

# menu

The first asparagus of the
season, cut just before
cooking and eating

Sweet potato fishcake
Garden salad leaves, fennel,
and saffron salad

Grapes
Mountain cheese
Home-baked sourdough loaf

LEFT: From field to plate in
a matter of minutes, the
first asparagus is a time of
celebration for the food-lover.
Simply roast or steam and
serve with melted butter or
vinaigrette.

RIGHT: The beauty of the
food—the intense purple of
the grapes, the tender hues of
the asparagus—is decoration
enough for this outdoor feast.

# A Colonnaded Loggia

What is it about eating in small buildings in the garden that is so thrilling? Is it the same excitement we found as children? Don't we all have a memory of sitting in that dark, secret place in the shrubbery, too small for an adult to crawl in, and devouring an odd selection of delectable morsels raided from the larder—and all the more delicious for that? Grandiose or ramshackle, I can't see a loggia, a summer-house, even a shed, without planning a feast.

This shady colonnaded loggia hidden in a leafy corner of the garden seemed to me the perfect place for four girls to meet on a hot summer's day. Removed from the shrill demands of the telephone and family, the cool loggia provided a sanctuary for shared confidences, and time to linger and lounge over an unpretentious lunch served informally on a low table.

The loggia was beautifully airy, opening on to the garden with dappled sunlight shimmering through the colonnades, but the trellis provided a windbreak and that important touch of secrecy.

ABOVE: With lunch set on a tole painted table, and pillows on comfortable chairs, the possibilities for tucking your feet up, balancing a plate on your lap, and endlessly chatting are irresistible.

LEFT: I love using leafy plants to bring the outside seamlessly in.

When the garden is all around, I like to extend it in my decorating scheme. The lime-greens echo young leaves; the bitter chocolate-green, the leafy shadows. On a blistering summer's day, these colors give a pleasing sense of coolness.

I've brought the garden onto the table with a low arrangement of cow parsley, white lilac, and acid-green apples. The bright light of dappled sunlight is picked up in the white French porcelain pots and the linen napkins, and is defracted through the glinting glass goblets.

I kept the table center low because I feel this is an intimate and animated lunch where vases could impede the flow of conversation, or perhaps even be knocked over by exuberant gestures.

# menu

White almond gazpacho

Balsamic vinegar glazed cutlets of lamb, infused with
rosemary, bay, and garlic

Pavlova with raspberries, strawberries, and mulberries

BELOW LEFT: As this is a table for intimate chat and shared confidences, I kept the table centerpiece low so that the guests can lean across to each other without sending a vase flying!

BELOW: Green majolica plates complement the leafy theme and add impact to the color scheme, being tonally askance to the predominance of lime-green.

# Outdoor Living

Pleasantly languishing in the heat of Provence, I had arranged to cook lunch for some Parisian friends who were also staying in the region. The day before, they rang to say, rather awkwardly, that one of their mothers had arrived and would it be possible to include her in the party.

Now I had met this mother on a previous occasion in Paris. She is a rather grand woman who does not speak English on principle and, no matter how hot it was, would think of wearing nothing less than an elegant suit and shoes. I had liked her, however, and immediately abandoned my plans for a shorts-and-flip-flops lunch, followed by lounging by the pool.

I decided instead on a lunch in two parts on the cool veranda. Before dessert, we would move from the table to four sofas, where puddings and mint tea would be served and the afternoon could be spent in animated conversation.

LEFT: Four sofas facing each other across an old wooden trunk, graced with a vintage striped runner for this elegant occasion, allowed the conversation to flow into the late afternoon.

RIGHT: The vibrant colors on the cool, shaded veranda were in stark contrast to the bleaching heat of the Provençal sun outside.

# menu

Chilled Provençal tomato and
chive soup

Roasted St Pierre with
courgette frittata

Strawberry tart from the
local pâtisserie

Matinée coffee mousse

Mint tea

ABOVE LEFT: I alternated the napkins
at each place setting in blue and
pink to bring out the colors of the
tablecloth.

LEFT: The dinner service in blue and
white with gold rims combined
formality, in that it all matched,
with the lightness and prettiness
appropriate to lunch on the veranda.

RIGHT: I love using a round table for
a lunch of eight or ten people. The
guests all face each other and lively
conversation is bound to ensue.

In deference to the elegance and age of my eldest guest, I set a formal but pretty table in blue and pink. Tiny orchids adorned each place setting and a pot of beautiful pink hydrangeas was my centerpiece. The theme was floral but in a finely decorative, rather than overblown cottagey way.

Delicious puddings were served in delicate crystal with slender stems, and mint tea in blue-and-white fine china.

At five my guests left, politely thanking us for a charming afternoon. Freed of the constraints of being amusing in French, we raced off to the beach.

ABOVE: The baby Phalaenopsis were so small that I put them in egg cups and placed one at each setting.

LEFT: A crisp white wine and carafes of water were the perfect antidote to the scorching heat beyond the shade of the veranda.

RIGHT: The French pâtisseries are so good that few French deign to make their own puddings. Following their lead, I bought the strawberry tart at the local pâtisserie (why, outside France, are such places few and far between?) but couldn't resist making coffee mousse to serve in these elegantly tall and fine champagne coupes.

# The Almond Grove

We had been at the beach all morning, friends with children and dogs, swimming and enjoying the glorious day. Suddenly it seemed a terribly bad idea to have lunch at the house! Still sandy and salty, we dropped wet towels and bathers in a heap, seized a brightly striped rug, shoved plastic plates and glasses into a basket, hastily assembled sandwiches from whatever goodies we could find in the refrigerator, whistled for the dogs, and set off to a cool, shady almond grove.

ABOVE: Always grab a few "unnecessaries" for impromptu picnics. It's fun to decorate your picnic spot and make it your own with Chinese lanterns and a string of bunting.

LEFT: Use spots, stripes, pillows, and throws, and masses of color.

# menu

Prawns with parasols

Emmental and tomato sandwiches
Lambs lettuce, avocado and asparagus salad
Roasted tuna salad with freshly squeezed (and picked)
lemon juice

Madeleines with chocolate cherries and orange peel
Ensaïmada
Fruit off the tree

Fresh orange and lemon juice

ABOVE LEFT: Blossom for scent, fruit for pudding. Add to your feast
with whatever you can forage.

LEFT: A rustic loaf, Ensaïmada cake, and lemons, plucked from the
garden tree as the party dashed out of the gate.

ABOVE RIGHT: Spots and stripes in brilliant poster paint colors are
just right for this jolly occasion.

ABOVE FAR RIGHT: Umbrella food cloches will keep the flies off the
madeleines. Try to keep picnic kit together to ensure a quick getaway
when the impulse takes you.

BELOW RIGHT: Good ripe tomatoes and Emmental cheese make the
most excellent sandwiches for a picnic.

BELOW FAR RIGHT: I don't want to worry about breaking things and
I hate plastic food containers. Cheerful plastic children's baskets are
brilliant for packing all sorts of stuff.

LEFT: Prawns with parasols? Whatever next? Whatever you can come up with, I say.

BELOW: Leave your best crystal at home in case you break it. These blue plastic sundae glasses create just the right mood.

BELOW RIGHT: Picnics allow everyone to let their guard down. Even those who would baulk at arranging flowers for a formal table will happily pluck a few stems and stick them in a plastic basket for a picnic rug.

I rather enjoy building up a little stash of unbreakable, portable bits and pieces that can be hurled into a basket as you rush out of the door on impulsive moments like this.

Having found the perfect spot for a picnic, I adore creating the scene and making a fun meal out of a bit of this and that. Spotted cocktail parasols stuck in a pot of prawns create a lovely Alice-in-Wonderland touch, and gathering a few wild flowers to adorn your rug is the perfect idle picnic task.

Nothing should be arduous in the least. There are those who like to do nothing more than snooze under a newspaper, and those who like to mosey around, discovering the perfect tree for a seat, or a clump of wild flowers. All manner of things should be allowed on picnics.

# Winegrower's Picnic

My good friend has a vineyard in southern Spain. Situated at the foot of mountains and surrounded by cypresses and olive trees, it is a truly beautiful place to go and stay.

When he told me he wanted to provide drinks and snacks for the workers as a thank you for completing a lengthy but essential stint of work—tying up all the young vines—I was very glad to help.

Any formality would have been quite wrong here with the vineyard workers still dusty after a day hard at it in the scorching sun.

After a day of battling with my garden, I like to sit under a tree with a glass of wine and a delicious snack and admire what I've done. My dog, Poppy, will usually sit at my feet, equally weary, having been busy getting under my feet all day!

This experience was my inspiration. I set up the wooden table on the edge of the vineyard where the workers could congratulate themselves on the fruits of their labor while enjoying fortifying refreshments, a big glass of local brandy, and cheerful chat with their fellow workers.

BELOW LEFT: We provided tapas. There was no need for knives or forks, just lots of freshly baked bread to mop up the delicious olive oil and juices.

BELOW: We fetched fortifying brandy from a local supplier who filled up our enormous flagon. I find that local drinks always taste most delicious in their own milieu.

BELOW: Red and yellow peppers were marinated in virgin olive oil and lemon juice. As I carried them down, I snatched a handful of oregano from the garden to tear over the top.

RIGHT: Rather optimistically, my friend brought down a chair and a straw hat to tip over his eyes should there be a moment to relax. The work was hard; there wasn't a respite!

BELOW RIGHT: This rustic picnic needed no frills. The beauty of the yellow ceramic dishes and the weathered basket and flagon lay in their fitness for the job at hand.

# menu

Chorizo
Manchego cheese
Home-grown olives
Roasted peppers with oregano
Rustic bread

Local brandy

LEFT: These painted metal chairs had been around on the farm for years and no-one is quite sure where they came from! They would be quite at home in the kitchen of a fashionable city apartment.

RIGHT: Good salty olives, a glass of brandy, and a stunning view. What could be better!

# Under the Palms

I once had the misfortune of being one of a party staying at the holiday home of a terribly nice couple who were so assiduous in their entertaining that we ended up being marshalled around from dawn til dusk like a troop of reluctant boy scouts.

When my friend lent me his house in Spain, I determined that I should not make the same mistake!

I decided to make lunch a supremely casual affair. Food should always be provided of course, but my guests need not stay if they were energetically engaged elsewhere. If they did attend, then gazing at the view, a good book on hand, and some idle chat should be the order of the day.

LEFT: I can rarely do without flowers and it took little planning to pick up this pretty pot of pinks from the garden and set it on the table.

RIGHT: An idle lunch: chunks of watermelon, excellent chilled soup (made the day before), rustic bread, and a reliable local wine.

So that my guests should not feel obliged to stay for lunch by catching glimpses of me slaving over a hot stove in the morning, I prepared meals that could feed three or ten with little effort but much deliciousness—chilled soup made in advance, bread, and fruit.

I chose a secluded lunch spot under the palms, in the shadow of an ancient stone wall where the view was endless. I heaped pillows on comfortable old chairs and covered the low table with an old poncho. Don't ask me why! It just hit the mood perfectly.

The table setting was not elaborate—all had to be brought down from the house in baskets—but I placed a pot of pinks on the table, opened a bottle of good local red wine, and our lazy lunch was complete.

BELOW LEFT: The table setting was charming but simple as everything had to be carried down from the house in a basket.

BELOW: These little beakers, which could be stacked in the basket, were perfect for the local, inexpensive red wine.

RIGHT: Entertaining is not always about hard work. It is important, above all, to make your guests feel comfortable.

## menu

Chilled zucchini and fennel soup
Rustic bread

Chunks of watermelon

CHAPTER FIVE

# Entertaining in Winter

# Thanksgiving Buffet

Wrap up warm, kick up your heels, and enjoy yourself is the moral of this story. Thanksgiving is being celebrated in upstate Vermont. It's November. The night is clear, cold, and starry but in a nineteenth-century hay barn, lit only by candles, fiddlers are playing, feet are stamping, and a barn dance is in full swing.

This traditional Thanksgiving supper takes the form of a generous picnic with organic wild turkey served in raffia boxes, buffet-style. The guests, weary for the minute of dancing, will settle down to eat with whom they like and where they like. The colors of the decorations are autumnal and suggested by the natural hues of the interior of the barn—straw, oak, and the olive-green painted benches. Abundant fruit and vegetables decorate the trestle tables—this is Thanksgiving, after all.

LEFT: The barn is lit solely by candles. Lanterns are hung at different heights from the ceiling, shedding their disparate glow over the abundant array of vegetables, reminding revelers why they celebrate Thanksgiving.

ABOVE: I love using candles and this candle setting, nestling snugly among fresh asparagus and glossy Swiss chard, holds a particular charm for me.

LEFT: Never forget the decorative potential of fresh fruit and vegetables. On occasions such as Thanksgiving or Harvest Festival, nothing could be more apt.

BELOW: I dyed napkins and tablecloths specifically for this occasion in saffron yellow, orange, and charcoal gray.

BELOW RIGHT: They may be simple fare, but freshly baked loaves of bread, with their appetizing aroma and gorgeous appearance, were essential for this feast.

I love exploring and using the relationship between food and flowers, and I never forget the decorative potential of food, particularly fruit and vegetables. Decorations of gorgeously fresh vegetables are perfect for a festival such as Thanksgiving. I dispensed with flowers altogether.

I heaped creamy florets of cauliflower in a shining bowl, and arranged acid-green grapes, tumbling over the edges of high vases, with heads of broccoli. I nestled squat church candles in glass dishes of crimson-veined Swiss chard and purple and green asparagus. Strawberries glowed scarlet in the candlelight in small baskets. Freshly baked rustic loaves were piled high. The feast was truly magnificent.

It was the fabulous idea of a few of my American friends to hold Thanksgiving as a barn dance and invite a hundred of their friends and family—quite a change from the conventional formal family dinner!

It is a good rule of etiquette, and makes the party much more fun, if you mingle and get to know new people. Barn dancing, of course, makes this almost unavoidable as you fly into the arms of this person and that.

At a shared party like this, do stay and help with the clearing up if you can. New friendships can be cemented over a pile of dirty dishes.

RIGHT: Look at your materials to find inspiration for your color scheme. Vegetables are not just green—look at the glowing red of the Swiss chard and the soft amethyst tones in the asparagus.

BELOW LEFT: Leaf-engraved glasses and open flagons of good red wine complete this Thanksgiving scene.

BELOW: Unfinished and unpolished, yet this centerpiece and lantern are perfect for a rustic celebration.

# menu

Squash soup with cinnamon
and bay

Roast wild turkey
with sage butter and onion gravy
Apple and sausage stuffing
Pan-tossed autumn vegetables
Candied sweet potato gratin

Apple pie with pecans
and dried cranberries
Pumpkin meringue pie

RIGHT: This brilliantly hued table
owes everything to nature: the colors,
the decoration. Bathed in gentle
golden candlelight, this is the perfect
Thanksgiving supper scene.

# Supper in the Library

Books can be found stacked hither and yon all over my house. Books to be pondered over, books to be studied, books for reference, and books to inspire—books are an essential part of my life.

So eating among them has to be one of my keenest pleasures. My library suppers are simple—a book in one hand, the other to eat—but delicious. I tend to favor freshly baked bread, a perfectly ripened cheese, and fruit.

A plate hastily cobbled together in the kitchen and balanced precariously on my knee just won't do either. Five minutes' attention to the table will make this plain supper a meal to savor and linger over, either with friends or alone.

LEFT: Table centers don't always have to be of an elaborate nature. Here I've gathered herbs from the garden and, on an inspired whim, scooped up a stone ornament. By placing them on the table with candles in soft oranges and greens, the mood is set.

RIGHT: A vintage plate and a linen napkin tied without fuss and adorned only with a small bundle of herbs are the details that finish the effect.

# menu

Freshly baked bread

Good-quality salty butter

English farm-produced cheese: Stilton and Cheddar

Celery

Apricots

A dependable Bordeaux

BELOW AND BELOW RIGHT: The cheese and bread are decorated with a good sprig of fresh sage. The dried apricots and celery are delicious accompaniments and at the same time pick up the soft colors of the candles.

RIGHT: This sturdy, rustically beautiful glass perfectly suits the comfortable, informal setting. I don't bother to raid my cellar for my finest wine. A dependable Bordeaux with deep notes of wood smoke and earth is just the thing.

# A Family Christmas

With my entire family gathering for Christmas at my Gloucestershire house, I created a fabulously festive table that diffused warmth, affection, wonder, and amusement for the perfect feast.

It was an occasion to use my most treasured and adored possessions, and to add a few surprises. I combined old and new, simple and costly, to enchant all my family. I gave free rein to caprice, setting a flock of knitted sheep to wander among the vintage crystal and bridge the seventy-year age difference between the youngest and oldest seated at the table. In such a setting, conversation was soon flowing, energy levels were rising, and a vital atmosphere was created.

LEFT: I love to bring greenery in from outside at this dark, yet opulent, time of year. A long garland of blue pine, scarlet roses, and festive berries brought the Christmas spirit to an already extravagant and lovely setting.

RIGHT: Folding your napkins to the center is a simple trick to get striped edges to the middle. A kindly local soul pinked and padded, stitched and sewed my Christmas puddings together in old-fashioned felt as an ornament for this occasion.

At Christmas more than any other time, I love to suffuse the whole house with a festive atmosphere so that my guests can bask in soft light and warmth with good things and the promise of more good things. My house becomes a radiant haven and we forget the dark, dreary weather outside.

The flickering light of candles illuminates the room, playing on the valuable old facet-cut crystal that I love to bring out at Christmas. Tinsel and glitter has its place but not here. Red roses and berries glow against the evergreens, while the flagons of claret have a gorgeous dark intensity against the white tablecloths and napkins.

The traditions of Christmas are all here and I make them beautiful in their essential simplicity. The excellent whole Stilton (God forbid the multiple choice of the cheeseboard!) is swathed in a white napkin and elegantly decorated with a sprig of sage. The wine and port are served in fine old crystal, and mince pies are offered on a cake-stand.

LEFT: I arranged the candles right up high or right down low so as not to interrupt the vivacious exchange of banter up and down and across the table that, in my family, is bound to ensue. The smiling knitted sheep will keep the children entertained as the decanter of rather good port is handed round to amuse the adults. At a gathering of very young, very old and in-between, it is great fun and quite a challenge to create a table that will appeal to all.

# menu

Quail's egg and Osetra caviar tartlet

Roast goose
Forcemeat stuffing
Brandy-soaked prunes
Braised red cabbage with Bramley apples
Brussels sprouts and chestnuts
Potatoes roasted in goose fat
Giblet gravy

Year-old home-made Christmas pudding
Brandy butter
Double cream

Stilton and port

LEFT: Benevolent cows gaze down from my painting at the fine display of Christmas victuals, arranged at different heights to intensify the scene of festive plenty.

RIGHT TOP AND BOTTOM: While not liking to stray too far from the venerable traditions of Christmas lunch, I do enjoy introducing something new—perhaps a tradition from another country. For my family Christmas, I served Italian jewel-like mostarda di frutta as a condiment from sparkling crystal comports.

# White Christmas

The crystalline glitter of icy days is celebrated in this fresh approach to a Christmas table, with a moss-green theme suggesting the first green shoots of early spring bulbs thrusting through sun-dappled snow.

An elegantly symmetrical table of glinting crystal and white napkins creates a delightfully playful scene with snowy owls, squirrels, long-necked deer, and frost-rimmed toadstools. Light flickering from candles animates the brilliance of the setting, creating movement and warmth in this winter wonderland.

ABOVE: I adore it when the atmosphere of a Christmas party is such that it just can't be contained and radiates out from the table to other parts of the room. This exquisite arrangement of animals and evergreen foliage, which adorns the fireplace, reminds us how truly beautiful winter can be.

LEFT: Ornate, beaded candlesticks and elegant, arching deer are introduced to project color, form, and height to the center of the table.

# menu

Truffle-scented, horn of plenty mushroom and caramelized onion tartlet

Monkfish tails stuffed with thin slices of orange and thyme,
baked on a bed of finely sliced fennel
Roasted winter vegetables drizzled with balsamic vinegar
Vine-roasted cherry tomatoes

Orange and amaretto panettone

Coffee and the winter tazza

It may be cold outside but within I've created an atmosphere of *joie de vivre* and warmth. Gathering together little animals and birds, Christmas candies and cookies, I've created a dazzling midwinter scene to be enjoyed by all ages. The contemporary art on the wall serves to endorse the display of color on the table. Great fun is to be had by making each place setting individual in order to stimulate conversation and good humor among the guests.

Stunningly different, this light style is a great contrast to the heavy opulence of green, red, and gold. I just couldn't hold back here. This is one of those times when profusion and lavishness has to be the order of the day.

LEFT: Perfect crystal, facet-cut with an ingenious simplicity, gives a true feeling of luxury and quality to an already bristling collection of beautiful objects.

TOP RIGHT: The dashing red of the toadstool adds a vibrant punctuation mark to the otherwise cool color scheme. A little dot or squiggle of red on a white napkin, or a scarlet detail on some delicious little treat, helps to set the delicate composition, adding a touch of Christmas fire to the icy glisten of this table.

RIGHT: As guests join the table, each one is presented with a low, crystal tazza in which nestle delicious *bonnes nouches* and charming little decorative gewgaws.

# Glossary

## GOOD MANNERS

### The Art of Greeting

As people arrive, welcome them at the door, take their coats, and let the guest know where the cloakroom is. Furnish them with a drink and then introduce them to a couple of other guests, giving names and a little information about each to get the conversation started. If they are first to arrive, try not to leave them "dangling" in thin air but stay with them and chat.

If you are cooking, prepare as much as you can in advance, so that you can concentrate on looking after your guests.

As a guest, you should have responded to your invitation within no more than a week of receiving it. You should dress appropriately and bring a small gift for your host—flowers, champagne, or chocolate are good choices. Be punctual, but NEVER early. Ten minutes after the time of invitation is considered perfect.

### At the Table

Always make a table plan in advance. In an ideal world seat your guests next to someone they know and someone they don't, but are likely to find congenial.

Keep an eye on your table, make sure glasses are topped up, and dishes passed. If you notice conversation flagging, throw in a comment to start it up again.

As a guest, you should wait to be seated and start to eat only when your host starts. It is up to you to make conversation and look after your fellow guests by passing them dishes, water, and wine.

It is acceptable to leave food on your plate, but not to make a fuss about not liking it. If a different wine is served with each course, don't feel bound to drain the glass each time. A little wasted wine is preferable to a drunken guest!

Make a point of thanking your host as you leave. Write a thank-you letter within two days. If you know your host well, an e-mail or telephone call is also nice as you can chat about the evening.

## TABLE LINEN

The tablecloth is the foundation of your setting. Center it so that the creases run straight down the table. It should hang down about 12 inches (30 cm) all round. When you have finished using the tablecloth, deal immediately with stains and iron carefully for folding and putting away so that the creases are neat.

It is worth investing in good heavy cotton or linen in white as it can be bleached or boiled to remove heavy staining. Napkins should be folded into a neat rectangle, or rolled and placed in a napkin ring or tied attractively. If you place the napkin on the plate, it makes it quite clear whose is whose and adds to the decoration of the setting. If the first course is already on the table, place the napkin on the left of the forks.

Unfold your napkin once seated and place it on your lap. At the end of the meal, don't refold it but leave it on your place setting.

## CHINA

Unless you have acres of storage space and tons of money, it is advisable to invest in one good dinner service, perhaps in cream or white, which can be dressed with napkins, trimmings, flowers, and tablecloths to achieve very different table decorations.

For dinner, your essentials are dinner plates, salad plates and side plates, soup bowls, pudding bowls and pudding plates, and coffee and tea cups and saucers. Some of these pieces can double as cereal bowls for breakfast, and cake plates for high tea. You will also need a tea-pot, a milk jug and a sugar bowl, and a butter dish.

Side plates should be placed to the left, all others in the center. All dishes from each course should be cleared from the table before the next is served.

CRYSTAL

The basic crystal requirement is a set of water glasses, a set of red wine glasses and smaller glasses for white wine, a set of champagne flutes and two good water jugs. Decanters, port glasses, sherry glasses, brandy glasses, and cocktail glasses may be added according to your tastes and habits.

When setting the table, the water glass should be placed on the right of the place setting above the knife. The other glasses should be placed in a row to the right of the water glass in order of use: white wine for the first course, red for the second, and so on. If the row is too long, make a v-shape.

CUTLERY/FLATWARE

It's worth investing in a good canteen of cutlery. Even if you look rather odd, it's a good idea to pretend to eat with it before you buy it. There's nothing worse than a knife-handle which is too thin to be held comfortably in the hand.

Each place setting should include a large knife and fork, a smaller knife and fork for salad and cheese, a dessertspoon and fork, and a teaspoon. You may also add soup spoons and butter knives.

Place cutlery so that you work from the outside in: the smaller knives and forks for the first course on the outside and the larger for the main course next to the plate. The soup spoon should go on the right with the knives. Line them up so that the bottom of the handles are in a straight line. Pudding spoons and forks can be placed above the plate or at the inside nearest the center of the setting down the sides, it's a matter of choice. A butter knife is set on the side plate.

Once you have finished eating, the knife and fork should be placed together with the handles toward you and prongs upward. In the United States, they should be placed diagonally across your plate with the handles at 4 o'clock.

## FLOWER VASES

The first thing to remember about vases and flower arrangements is that they should not hinder conversation between guests on opposite sides of the table.

If vases are tall, they should be slender and placed down the center of the table at intervals with good spaces between. An elaborate table center should be kept below eight inches in height.

For special parties, an individual flower can decorate each place setting. Use tiny crystal shot glasses or even old port glasses, they need not match.

Crystal vases give the impression of light and space but also show the flower stems and water, so make sure these are impeccable.

Avoid overcrowding your table with flowers. Remember that you need to leave space for side plates, glasses, and serving dishes.

## FLOWERS

Flowers be bought the day before so they are "a point" but should only be placed on the table just before your guests arrive so that they are as fresh as possible. They are the last step in setting the table and bring it to life.

Use flowers to bring out the colors on your table and add height, or as a low centerpiece. Your arrangements will clinch the mood. Consider buying bunches of white roses or orchids for formal dinners and gathering bunches of garden flowers for less formal occasions.

Save scented flowers for the hall or sitting-room. On a dining table, the scent will wrestle with the flavors of the food.

# Index

# Acknowledgments

Looking back on the year that this book has taken to come to fruition, it seems to me that I have many long-suffering friends, family, and colleagues! Books are hard work, but also very rewarding, and I should like to share that feeling of reward with those who put up with me and my mess! Encouragement and enthusiasm have come from so many quarters that it is hard to list in an accurate way all who have shown their kindness. I must, however, particularly thank the following people whose unstinting generosity has, without question, been the backbone of this project.

Paul Ryan, who has been a total delight to work with and who, as you have seen, clearly has a great talent

Joseph and Isabel Ettedgui
Colin Orchard
Fred and Suzanne Rheinstein
Courtnay and Terry Daniels
Tim and Dana Jenkins

Barbara Bergman and Klas Kall
Tricia Guild
Nicola and Tony Schlesinger
Samantha Kingcome
Alex and Charlie Manners

I should also like to thank:

Mint
Colin Hawkins
Terence Barry
Victoria Brotherton
Susan Crewe
Caroline and David Dickinson
Kevin and Caroline Weaver
Marc and Heather Weaver
Loxi Greenfield
Sarah Harger
Rupert Thomas
Sandra Canales
Aida Reyes
Sarah King
Mariavera Chiari Architetto
Joe Trinanes
Michael Nicholson
Jess Brown
Jenny South
Nina Campbell
Gary Cooper
Anita Patel
Carol Paul

Fay Cariaso
Paul Bramfitt
Lisa Gibson Keynes
Nicholas Carter
Haley Felchin
Darren Shick
Posy Gentles
Eric Salatin
Brian Freidman
Christine Wood
Doresa Jones
Polly McConnell
Jan Whitten
Dan Whitten
Ricky Jones
Morris

And of course my long-suffering sparring partner and publisher, Cindy Richards, whom I thank for her vision, enthusiasm, trust, and continued support.

For further information on William Yeoward, visit:
www.williamyeoward.com
www.williamyeowardcrystal.com